From:

MY LOVE,

You Were...

A celebration of you
and your awesomely one-of-a-kind YOU-ness!

you were a fragrance,

you'd smell like

_____

&

_____ .

you were a dessert,

you'd be

_____ .

you were

a beautiful place,

you'd be

_____.

you were a holiday,

you'd be

_____

because

_____.

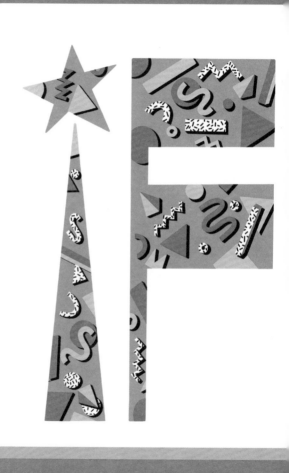

you were a color,

you'd be

_____.

you were

a warm beverage,

you'd be

_____

because

_____.

they made a movie

of your life,

_____

&

_____

could play you and me.

you were

a magical spell,

you'd conjure up

_____,

like poof!

you were

a classic album,

you'd be

_____.

you had

a stand selling

your charm & your

_____,

you'd be rich (maybe)!

you were

a swear word

or exclamation,

you'd be

_____.

you were

a new dance craze,

you'd be

even sexier than the

_____

for sure.

you were a medicine,

you'd be

_____

because you cure my

_____ !

you ran the world,

there'd be more

_____

and less

_____ .

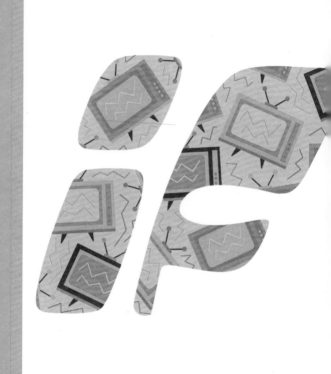

you were

an old-timey device

or technology,

you'd be

_____.

you were

a wild animal

doing something funny

in a YouTube™ video,

you'd be

_____

_____ .

you were

a board game,

you'd be

_____.

you were

a librarian, you'd be

in charge of the

_____

section.

you were

a flower,

you'd be a

_____.

you dressed up as

_____

for Halloween,

I'd 100% be

_____ .

we could do anything

on a dream date,

I'm pretty sure

you'd want to

_____.

you were

a punctuation mark,

you'd be

_____.

you were

a buried treasure chest,

you'd contain

_____

(and maybe

_____).

you and I

were together

in a past life,

I bet we

_____.

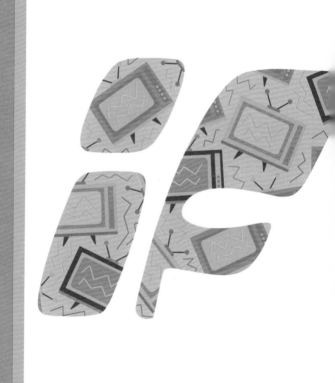

you were

a standup comedian,

your catchphrase

would be

"_____

_____."

you were

a superhero,

your superpower

would be

_____.

you were

a planet or celestial body,

you'd be

_____.

you were

any hotter,

there might be

_____!

you were

willing to

_____

with me, I'd be so

_____ .

you weren't my

_____,

life would be

a whole lot less

_____!

Wherever you go

and whatever

you want to do, try,

or become...

I love you!

Created, published, and distributed by Knock Knock
6695 Green Valley Circle, #5167
Culver City, CA 90230
knockknockstuff.com
Knock Knock is a registered trademark of Knock Knock LLC

ISBN: 978-168349433-1
UPC: 825703-50311-1

10 9 8 7 6 5 4 3 2 1

MIX
Paper from
responsible sources
FSC® C139034